# Bread Making Mastery for Beginners

## Perfect Dough Alchemy

By

Rebecca Scott

**CSB Academy Publishing Company.**
P.O. Box 966
Semmes, Alabama 36575

Cover & Interior designed
By
Angie Anderson

*First Edition*

# WHAT'S IN THIS BOOK

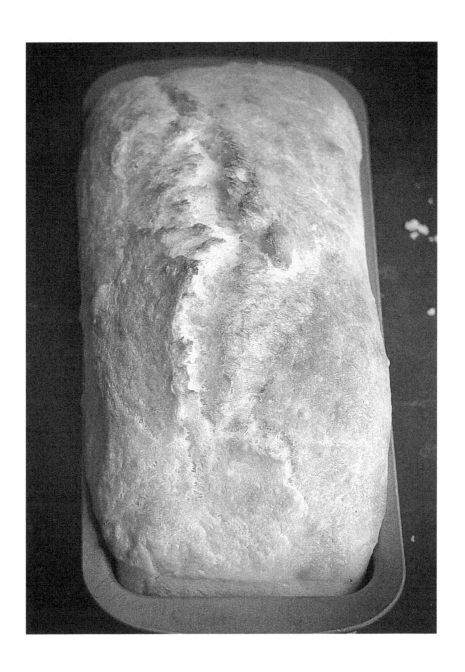

# INTRODUCTION

Everyone loves bread. And everyone loves warm homemade bread.

In this country, we love bread so much that we make bread bowls for salads we eat as well as with soups. And when you have that soup in the bread bowl there's nothing better than to dip chunks of bread into the soup.

And that's even explaining our emotional attachment to bagels, pita bread, and flatbreads. I am sure you can probably add a few more of your favorite bread to this short list as well.

So why, given such a love affair aren't there more people making homemade, customized bread? Why are we settling for commercially made bread that seems to be made with less fiber than ever before and more ingredients that are impossible to pronounce, let alone know what they are?

One reason there aren't more of use "bread bakers" out there is because of fear. Yes, most of us – and I was one – at some point consider making fresh bread, then stop dead on the tracks. Why?

One word: **Yeast.**

Okay perhaps not the yeast itself, but how you must handle bread dough after you've added the yeast

And once again that only takes one word to answer: Knead.

If you're like so many others, you see a delicious-looking recipe, start to read it, only to find it takes yeast and – yikes! – kneading. That's when you turn the page as quickly as possible. Here's more my speed, you say, "No bake peanut butter cookies."

You may believe I'm exaggerating and I am a bit to make my point. But when it comes to some individuals, I've come closer to the truth than some would care to admit.

The truth of the matter was, I was more like that several years ago. Honestly, if anyone had told me that someday I'd be writing a short, how-to book on baking bread successfully, I would have laughed on their face. "You have me confused with someone who enjoys baking," I'd tell them.

Today, mere short years later I am known to my family and my inner circle of friends as the "bread baker." What's more, when anyone I know is trying to bake bread for the first time, they inevitably call me. I either talk them through their nervousness or lack of self-confidence or I explain to them how to "fix" a mistake.

You might be asking yourself how did I get to this point in my life that the words *yeast* and *knead* don't cause panic? In fact, when I hear them, I get giddy. I like to think I'm a child again, playing in a sandbox, getting lost in my own world.

## WHAT STARTED ME ALONG THIS ROAD?

I first considered baking bread at home when buying it for the family became an overwhelming chore. For most people buying bread is nothing more than racing down the bread aisle of your neighborhood grocery store and picking up a loaf of bread for the week. At most, two loaves if that French or Italian bread looked extremely good and fresh.

Then somewhere along the way buying bread became a major event. People would look in my cart see the four or five loaves of bread and ask if we were expecting a major weather disaster which I was preparing for. Oh, I wish I could have lied and said yes.

But, I couldn't merely answer no and hoped no one would try to press me on the issue. I used to buy one of those super cheap, white bland loaves of bread for my husband and my oldest teenage son, a gluten-free loaf for my teenage daughter. Or, that low-carb bread to satisfy the keto diet of my other teenage son.

The cost alone was ridiculous, but I was always able to rationalize this by just saying that my family's particular health problems were being taken care off. Then, one day someone had mentioned the amount of sugar found in refined white bread. Then, on one trip I tried to buy whole wheat bread with the most fiber. Imagine my shock and dismay when I found very few types of bread had much fiber to begin with, and the cost of those breads were through the roof!

And then someone finally suggested that I should try to make my own bread. The cost, considering what I was spending in a week for essential was ground wheat with no health benefits.

As I thought about it for a while, decided it couldn't be any more insane than what I was doing now. So I gave it a shot. The first try left something to be desired, but my family seemed to like it and encouraged me to keep trying. And as I did, I had to admit that I was getting better at making bread. Soon the numbers of loaves I bought in comparison to those that I made dwindled. Today, my family eats nothing but homemade bread.

The really cool thing is that it doesn't take much more than a tweak in a recipe here or a small change in order to make basically the same bread acceptable to my daughter's gluten-free diet, my son's low carb regimen.

So, in a nutshell, that's how I overcame my fear of yeast, my phobia of kneading and my dependence on the store-bought bread. Everyone has within them, a point at which they turn a corner and never look back. Mine just happened to deal with bread making at home.

## WHAT THIS BOOK MEANS TO ME

I wrote this book hoping that when you were ready to bake your own bread, I could be with you so to speak. This book is meant to be the voice on the other end of the phone call, explaining how to get you through that first kneading session or that first mixing of your ingredients or even explaining what some of the cryptic baking terms meant.

In a nutshell, I'm providing you exactly what I wish I always had when I first started. A friendly environment where none of my questions were seen as too stupid to ask.

I've put as much information together as I thought you might need, without going off on tangents about the chemical reactions of bread ingredients. In the beginning, it's more important to get the proper steps down and perform them correctly. Then, if after you want to investigate more about the scientific side of the baking process, then by all means do so.

I talk briefly about the advantages and disadvantages of making bread with or without a bread machine, as well as the health benefits you can receive from eating loaves that come straight out of your oven.

In this book, I discuss all the bread baking equipment you may need, so you can take into account what you have and what you will need from the very beginning. But wait, there's more. And the "more" includes a quick primer on kneading as opposed to the pull and fold method of mixing the gluten of the dough around. In addition to word descriptions of both of these methods, I've pointed you to what I consider are some of the best YouTube videos I can find that show you how to do these vital steps.

There are even chapters on some of the best tips for troubleshooting bread baking problems before they turn into disasters and a sample recipe to get you started as well as an assortment of recipes so you can bake just about anything from French bread, to a form of pita-like (unleavened bread) bread rolls.

When all is said and done – and baked – I hope you enjoy this hobby half as much as I do. Let's get started reading. There's no time like the present!

# CHAPTER 1: WHAT ARE THE REAL BENEFITS OF HOMEMADE AND STORE-BOUGHT BREAD?

Ah! Bread. The stuff of life. The stuff that keeps our body –and soul together.

What? Is it not viewed quite like this any longer?

In a way that's understandable. What with the growing concern over gluten found in almost all grains and the "genetically modified" crops, as well the additives and some ingredients that are not only impossible to pronounce but suspect to doing your body more harm than good.

Before we cover any of the health benefits or natural ingredients, we'd be remiss if we didn't remind you of the aroma of homemade bread fresh out of the oven. It's a fragrance that lasts a lifetime in your memory (like it did in my mind). That in itself is a reason to bake your own bread.  Below is only a short list of some of the benefits associated with making your own bread

## THE COST OF HOMEMADE BREAD.

Some individuals argue that the cost of homemade bread is more expensive that some white bread found on sale. That's hard to argue with. But that's not a fair comparison either. There really are no health benefits in those giant loaves of white bread, made with refined flour stripped of any types of nutrients. White bread is bland to eat and tops the list of foods on the glycemic index, which indicates which foods spike your glucose the fastest.

Start buying something a cut above white bread and now you're beginning to see the true cost of bread. Wheat bread which has been touted as a much healthier bread has risen in cost over the years. But, then, I'm not telling you anything you don't already know.

And if you try to buy a baguette or a good loaf of French bread, you probably hesitate because of the cost. The cost, regardless of however much you love a particular type or even a type of roll, makes all of us give some thought to if we really need it or if it is worth splurging on.

# Six Key Benefits of Homemade Bread

## Homemade Bread is Healthier

There is less contention about this benefit. When you make your bread at home, you know exactly the ingredients and their quality.

The next time you're at the grocery store, check out for yourself the ingredient list for a loaf of bread. It doesn't matter whether you choose to read the list on white or wheat bread or any of your favorite types. In fact, go ahead and read them all. Before long you'll find they all have one thing in common. Additives and other unpronounceable substances that help to keep its shelf life high, but is of dubious quality when it comes to your health.

You don't have to worry when you make your own bread because you've put every ingredient in the mixing bowl yourself, you know how to pronounce each one because they're the ingredients used for cooking and baking every day.

## YOU CAN EASILY ADJUST THE CORE RECIPE

It's true. It only takes a tweak or two of the recipe in order to make a gluten-free version of a certain kind of bread. The ease with which you can adjust your base recipe to make it acceptable to nearly anybody is amazing. And while adjusting recipes for those who have an intolerance to gluten may be your first thought, your second should be carbohydrates.

Many individuals, for whatever reason, have to pay strict attention to the number of carbs they eat throughout the day. Making a low-carbohydrate version of bread is actually easier than what you may be led to believe by bread manufacturers. In this way, these carb-restricted persons can enjoy bread occasionally. They'll certainly be grateful for that.

## HOMEMADE BREAD ISN'T JUST FOR DAILY EATING

Not by a long shot! And you can take this advantage in several ways. So many people run to the store to see if they can grab a holiday specialty bread, whether for Easter or Christmas to name just two holidays.

When you make your own version of this holiday bread, you're not only eating bread that's heads and shoulders above what you can buy, but you're saving precious time by politely bowing out of that long line.

But more than that, if you decide just to go and serve one of your regular homemade bread – nothing fancy – it will still make your meal a cut above the average meal. It's entirely your choice.

## Take Control of Your Health

We've already touched upon this in some other paragraphs, but this is the part of the book, where you can really sit up and take notice of the fact that you can get control of your health back.

Sometimes when you eat store-bought bread, you do so almost grudgingly. At least I did. Having done everything else in a day for the good of my health and yes for my weight, I felt like I was forced to give up a portion of my health, or worry about my weight so that I can have a slice or two of bread.

By eating store-bought bread, I'm at the manufacturer's whim on the amount of sweetener they used for activating the yeast, for starters. At the same time, I've lost control of how much salt in a slice of bread. When I make my own, I can change the salt in the bread to suit my own needs, not the whim of the commercial baker.

Why add all those unnecessary fats and dairy products? Commercial bread add these to boost the depth of flavor of the bread, as well as to make the bread look fluffier.

## WHAT'S IN THAT LOAF AGAIN? THE UNKNOWN INGREDIENTS

And I'm not just talking about the long list of additives that you may never discover why they're included. I'm talking about those other ingredients – the ones that don't show up on the label.

Don't believe me? A reporter attempted to obtain, not so very long ago, a list of additives that go into a certain brand of bread. The manufacturer refused to provide him with the entire list. Why? The food scientist at the firm said they couldn't disclose certain additives because they feared revealing trade secrets. True. There's no way I can make this up.

## THE MARKETING CLAIMS OF STORE-BOUGHT BREAD DON'T HOLD UP.

Many packages contain the comforting words, "made with whole grains" or even announce they're a wonder "multigrain" bread. Look through the ingredients label and you'll discover they're made with nothing more than white flour.

Fiber? What Fiber?

For the longest time, I would scan each loaf of bread on the shelf looking for the ones that contained the most fiber thinking I was promoting my health. Now, I've learned that most of the fiber of bread is due to cellulose, inulin or a few other empty-health additives.

When you make your own bread, you can be sure that it will have fiber thanks to the whole grains you put into it. This is the type of fiber you need to help keep some of those degenerative diseases at bay, especially heart disease and cancer.

# CHAPTER 2: HOW A BREAD MACHINE WORKS

The bread machine. There may never have been one kitchen appliance that has been the center of so much controversy. Appliance fads come and go, the George Foreman's grill, sandwich makers, salad shooters, even handy-dandy slicers, and dicers.

But the bread machine seems to ignite a certain ire among those who believe that making bread should be done by hand and never, ever by some machine.

The bread machine has the ability to do all the work of making fresh bread for you. The only thinking you need to do is to place the ingredients in the machine, flip a couple of appropriate switches and walk away. When you come back, you'll have warm fresh bread.

That's why so many people love it. It's also why so many people hate them. Before we delve into the advantages and disadvantages of using the machine, let's talk a bit about how it works.

The machine holds a removable tin which is where you'll place all your ingredients. It has a unique design with an axle. The axle is what connects the tin to the motor. And by the way, there's also a waterproof seal that lies between the tin and the axle to keep all the ingredients in the tin.

All you need to do is simply load your specific ingredients into the tin.

The real beauty of this machine is that it takes all the guesswork out of the process. And that is why so many people who believe baking bread is an art hate it. They refuse to believe that the making of great bread can be reduced to dumping ingredients into a tin and reducing it to an afterthought.

Some models even have a built-in memory as well as a delayed timer. This can come in handy when you set it to start sometime in the middle of the night and wake up in the morning to the smell of fresh homemade bread.

Here are the guidelines for using a "generic' model of the bread maker. The steps give you a general idea of how these machines work. If you have one, or will be getting one, then by all means you should follow the instructions that come with your machine.

This set of instructions merely helps to make you familiar with how the machines work.

Don't make any bread until you've read your machines instructions.

Take a few moments to find out the following:

- *What size loaf does it make?*

- *What are the cycles it goes through?*
- *Does it have control settings for the crust?*

Most bread machines make loaves as small as a pound and as large as three pounds, and they have upwards of ten different cycles.

A cycle in a bread machine refers to the process the bread machine will go through. The basic cycle, for example, may make only basic white bread. There may be a whole wheat cycle that bakes that type of bread.

Then there are the "dough cycles" which involved kneading the bread. You may find your machine has a cycle that might be labeled something akin to "crust control." You can use this setting if you want to decide how "light" or "dark" you'd like the crust to be.

As you can see, these compact machines really are self-confined baking ovens.

After you understand the knobs and controls, you can jump in to see how, according to some, it works its "magic."

By taking some time to familiarize yourself with your bread machine, you will know what you can do with it and what ingredients you'll want to prepare.

## 6 STEPS OF MAKING BREAD WITH A BREAD MACHINE

### 1. MEASURE ALL OF YOUR INGREDIENTS

Before you place your ingredients in your machine, be sure to measure them out as accurately as you can. Before you put these ingredients together, you'll get better-tasting bread if you let all these ingredients warm to room temperature.

Now you might overlook this "minor" detail and one you can ignore, but in reality, it's much more crucial than it appears. Room temperature ingredients mix together with greater ease than those that have just been plucked out of the refrigerator. There are a few bread machines that have a nifty feature that can detect when your ingredients hit room temperature and won't start the process – any process until the ingredients are warmer. And believe it or not, you'll be able to see the difference in your bread.

## 2. NOW YOU CAN ADD YOUR INGREDIENTS

Believe it or not, you'll have to add them in the proper order. Many of today's bread-baking machines will let you know what order they want the ingredients. Don't be surprised that not all machines want you to add these in the same order. Be sure to pay attention to the machine's instructions. But once you check for this, you can guess that many machines are in agreement about this order.

More often than not, you'll be adding the liquids first, then the dry ingredients and then finally the yeast. If the yeast comes in contact with the liquids, you'll have the fermentation process start too early, which can cause problems later on.

## 3. SELECT YOUR SETTINGS

Once you have the room-temperature ingredients in the bread machine in the proper order, you can begin to select the various settings.

Of course, the number and the variety of settings you need to choose depends on what your machine offers you. First, it'll ask you about the type of cycle you want to use. This can range anywhere from basic to express bake, dough and even cake and gluten-free.

If you're baking basic bread, you can expect the length of the baking process to take from one to three hours. You'll want to consult your owner's manual frequently the first several times you use your machine. It should be able to fill in many of the questions that pop into your mind right before you press those buttons. Keep in mind anything your owners' manual instructs you to do takes precedence over the generic directions here. That's the only way you can be sure of making great-tasting bread.

This is also where that setting for the consistency of the crust will be. Normally the options here include light, medium and dark crust. This is something, you'll not only adjust with the type of dough you're making, but you'll be adjusting it at the beginning to get an idea of what each setting produces.

## 4. NOW YOU CAN PRESS START

You may think we've been pressing a lot of buttons to get this far, and in a sense, we certainly have. But as you become familiar with your machine, you'll have what cycles you want down to a science. It'll all become second nature to you and won't take much time at all.

When you're first getting familiar with your make and model of the bread machine, going slowly and being deliberate and detailed is the best route to take.

When you hit the "start" button for the first time, you're probably going to be anticipating a combination of noises that indicate it's doing its job. After that, you're going to be able to breathe again, you think. You'll be pleased to hear the sound of the machine baking. I hate to burst your bubble, but if your machine is equipped with a timer to wait to mix until all the ingredients are at room temperature, it may be nearly an hour before you notice any action in your little "bread box." But don't worry, the action will occur, guaranteed.

If your machine comes with a "viewing window" you'll want to check on the progress once and a while. Okay, I'll be honest, most people check on it just because it's so much fun to see it work.

But this can also help you see what's happening and if you need to step in and take a moment of control. If you look and notice that the dough is sticking to the sides, then you'll want to stop the process, take a dough spatula and scrape the dough off the sides.

## 5. TAKE THE "KNEADING BLADE" OUT

Before the baking cycle even begins, check to see if you're able to remove what's referred to as the "kneading blade." By doing this, you're making sure it doesn't bake into the bottom of the bread. If it does, it's not a disaster and won't affect the flavor of the bread. But you will end up with an unappealing hole in your bread.

## 6. REMOVE THE BREAD

Once the bread is done, then you'll want to take it out of the machine immediately. This may sound urgent, but it's urgent for a good reason. To do this, you'll want take the pan out of the machine, if possible. You'll want to be sure to use oven mitt. The pan will still be hot.

This will prevent the crust from getting any harder. Many of the newer machines now come with a "keep warm" option. While it will definitely retain the freshness of your loaf of bread, but the sooner you remove the loaf the better the bread will taste.

You'll want to set the bread on your cooling rack. This allows the water molecules inside escape from the bread. The result is a loaf of bread that isn't soggy, but still retains the moisture and the soft texture we all love.

And whatever else you do, be sure you let the bread to cool before you try to slice it. If you don't, you'll find you end up with one squished mashed up lump of bread. Delicious as even that may be, it won't look appetizing and it'll be quite difficult to eat!

If your machine doesn't have this function, allow yourself enough time by taking the ingredients out ahead of time. When measuring out your ingredients, make sure your measurements are accurate. Don't add more or less than what the recipe calls for. This is really important as the slightest error will ruin the texture, taste, and appearance of the bread.

Is bread made in a machine better than bread made by hand? The answer to that depends on who you ask. And it's the topic of the next chapter.

# CHAPTER 3: THE FACEOFF: BREAD MADE BY HAND VERSUS BREAD MACHINE

The "controversy" rages on.

Okay, so it's not quite a controversy, but when you get two or more bread-baking hobbyists together, you'll likely to find them in a lively discussion about the advantages and disadvantages of baking by hand or by using a bread baking machine.

If you've never baked bread or never used a bread machine, you may be asking the same thing yourself. So before delving too far into the details of this hobby, let's take a long view at the hobby itself.

Baking homemade bread by hand has many benefits, as its proponents will enthusiastically tell you. Here are only a few of the many advantages to baking homemade bread without using the machine.

## 4 DISADVANTAGES OF BREAD MACHINE

## 1. WHEN I BAKE THE BREAD IN THE MACHINE, THE LOAF TURNS OUT MISSHAPEN

When you bake the dough in the bread machine, you're "stuck" with an awkward shape to your loaf. Many times the corners and the bottom edges of the "loaf" are rounded.

A bread machine was created originally to ensure that during the mixing and kneading portions of the process in order there would be no extra flour left why you're kneading the dough and place it into a traditional bread pan.

Many times the corners and the bottom edges of the bread, after it bakes in the machine are more rounded and to be truthful doesn't really resemble any bread that you would find in a bakery.

This criticism may sound like a minor issue. And it is, if your family doesn't mind the shape of the shape of the bread. But if you're going to give the bread away you would like it to look as professional (and normal) as possible.

## 2. THERE ARE HOLES IN THE CRUST ON THE SIDE OF THE DOUGH BAKED IN A MACHINE

Many individuals may find this not at all upsetting, but for others, it's a major complaint. The holey texture of the crust, in fact, affect the taste as well. The crust is tough to chew. It's not nearly as tender as the all-handmade bread.

## 3. HOLES ON THE BOTTOM OF THE BREAD

You may never have noticed these holes before or if you have, not have known what caused them. Some people overcome this disadvantage simply by removing the dough from the machine and then, take out the blades. They replace the dough and allow it to bake in the machine –sans the blades. It will rise one more time, and then you bake it in the machine with no stress about the holes.

You may still find you have holes in the bottom of the bread, but at least this time they'll be much smaller.

## 4. YOU DON'T HAVE CONTROL THE LENGTH OF TIME THE BREAD BAKES IN THE MACHINE

This is a major complaint for many bakers. While it would be problematic for most of us who like to peek into the oven to check on something baking or cooking, it's even more so with any project that contains yeast.

Yeast is a living, thriving organism. This is a fact that we all tend to forget or overlook from time to time. And it's a large part of the reason experienced bread bakers fear to let go of the control over this process. The reaction of yeast is dependent on the ingredients in your bread and the temperature surrounding the dough.

The machine, with its built-in timer, isn't constructed to make allowances for these variables. The machine is created so it automatically goes to the bake cycle regardless of whether the bread is fully risen or not. If the dough hasn't risen because it's a bit colder and draftier in your kitchen than usual, you could find that your loaf of bread is smaller and heavier than you'd like.

Or if the dough is too warm, then the bread will rise before it's time. This may also occur if your recipe contains a great deal of sugar in it. The final product may rise, only to take a dip. And the bread looks like its poor spine is broken.

The problem is exacerbated if you bake with whole grains. The rising times on these breads are for the most part lengthier. While, some machines have dedicated whole wheat cycles they run automatically and may not work exactly as you'd like.

## WHY PEOPLE WOULD FIGHT SOMEONE WHO WANTED TO TAKE THEIR BREAD MACHINES FROM

Just as you find individuals who aren't the least bit impressed or excited about using a machine when making their homemade bread, you'll find others who swear they'd be lost without them.

And don't even suggest to these people that you'll just take their machine – more than likely you'll have a fight on your hands. What makes them so dedicated to their machines?

Below are just a few more popular reasons. As you continue baking bread, you may find yourself in this group.

## 3 KEY ADVANTAGES OF BREAD MACHINE

### 1. IT'S EASIER

Or as one of my friends said, "There are less mess and far less fuss." With the help of a bread machine, the extent of getting the delight and health benefits of eating homemade bread come down to measuring out ingredients, putting them into the bread pan, pressing a few buttons (oh, my did I just break a nail?) and then waiting for the delicious results.

When it comes to clean up, all you need to do is wash the bread pan and the small blade. It doesn't get any better than this.

### 2. SAVE TIME AND EFFORT

All that is required of you is a ten-minute commitment. Yes, I said ten minutes. Now look at some recipes where you knead the bread two or three times. The preparation time alone for some of these recipe is more than ten minutes.

By the time you're prepared to actually start putting the ingredients together, you could be, with the help of a bread machine, already in the living room reading a book waiting for the smell of fresh bread to waft throughout the house.

## 3. THE BREAD MACHINE BAKES EVEN WHEN YOU CAN'T

Do you have limited time between coming home from work and soccer practice, but you're still craving warm homemade bread? If you had a bread machine, the answer could be as simple as putting your ingredients in the machine and flipping the switch before you leave the house. When you get home, you'll be walking into a house with the sweet scent of warm bread beckoning you to come, sit a while and enjoy.

Perhaps you're going to place the ingredients in before you go to work. Now, that's something to keep you smiling all day long.

Who wouldn't want to wake up to the smell of freshly baked bread? Short of hiring Martha Stewart or even the baker from your favorite bakery shop to prepare fresh bread for you in the morning, it's still possible. And you just have to look at the timer on your bread machine. Of course, you better set that coffee pot at the same time. Now, there are two irresistible enticements to get up in the morning.

# CHAPTER 4: STANDARD OPERATING EQUIPMENT FOR THE PERFECT LOAF OF BREAD

One of the first pieces of equipment you'll need is a mixer, preferably one that sits on its own stand. If you have an older model, one that has seen you through some good baking memories, keep it as long as it works. Don't run out and spend money on one of those top-end mixers. Unless you have your mind set on one and this is the only way you can talk yourself into purchasing one.

What you will need to dig out if you don't know its current location is a dough hook that came with the stand mixer. This is a bent or curved attachment (Yes, it does look "hook-like!") And, yes, this attachment actually kneads the dough quite quickly and definitely in an efficient manner. It's good to have because, as opposed to you doing it on your own, you won't end up with flour all over the countertop area. Imagine that!

The dough hook is an excellent attachment to have because when it kneads the dough, it ensures gluten develops rapidly. Gluten, if you didn't know, is the protein in the wheat dough which makes it pliable and keeps the air bubbles on the inside of the loaf. This way, you'll end up with fluffy, chewy bread.

## DIGITAL SCALE

Why?

Believe it or not, but the perfect bread dough depends on its ratio of flour to water. Sure, you can measure this all out in cups, as recipes carefully have you do, but you'll find your bread will be consistently better tasting the more accurate your ratio is.

Converting your bread recipe from cups to weights isn't that difficult at all. Simply measure out your flour in a cup. Weigh it. Record this weight. Repeat this two more times. Then take the average of these three weights, by adding the three results together and dividing by three. Now you have the weight of an "average" cup of water.

You also know that if your recipe calls for seven cups of flour, you'll need 30.8 ounces of flour weighed out on the scale.

## DOUGH SPATULA AND BENCH SCRAPER

Many begin their hobby being selective of the equipment they think they're going to need. I've had people come up to me and say, "You were right. I can't think of making bread without my dough spatula and bench scraper." If you're not familiar with the process of baking bread, you wouldn't have a clue why I prize these two items so much.

The dough spatula is, without a doubt, my "weapon" of choice when I transfer the dough from one bowl to another. It's also my "go-to" piece of equipment when I mix the dough by hand. Its mission is to make sure not one shred of dough is left behind. And it's serious about its job. I highly recommend it.

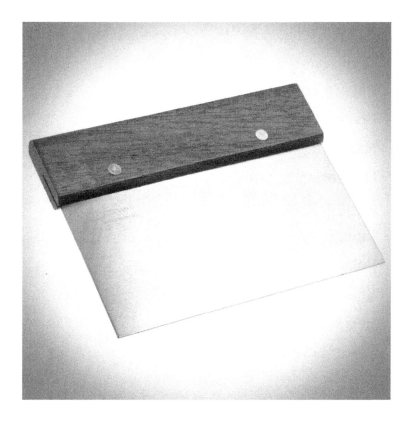

A bench scraper is a wonderful tool in order to make sure you retrieve as much dough as possible from your cutting board or another working surface. If you've ever watched any food recipe show, you know exactly what they look like (Look at the image above).

They're flat, usually steel, with a reticular surface and a large "handle" at one end. You can use these for just about everything you make.

## OTHER ESSENTIAL TOOLS

- Baking sheets
- Bread Pans
- Measuring cups, dry and liquid
- Measuring spoons
- Mixing bowls, two large
- Ruler
- Rolling pin
- Saucepan, medium-sized
- Serrated knife
- Thermometer
- Timer
- Wire cooling rack
- Wooden spoon, large or long-handled

# CHAPTER 5: WALKING THROUGH PARTS OF A STANDARD RECIPE

It's best if you've never baked bread before, to begin with, an easy standard recipe. Don't worry, while at first your taste buds and enthusiasm are telling you to jump into some wonderfully creative loaf, stick with the basics first.

It's much more satisfying to have the aroma of fresh bread wafting through your home on your first try than to have a disappointing attempt at a type of bread that's beyond your basic understanding. And have to put up with your family's jokes about calling the fire department to get that burnt smell out of your house.

But even before we start the basic recipe, I thought you might want a quick introduction to some of the terms you may run across as well as what to do with your dough during and after you put them to mix together.

I never imagined some of these steps when I first started. I quite literally stared at the recipe for a while before I felt enough self-confidence to start or to move to the next level. While it may have been a comical sight, it was not in any way a pretty sight. If I can help you prevent you this confusion, then I figure I'm doing my job.

Whenever you feel lost, or you've lost your self-confidence building your loaf, you can always come back to this section of the chapter and check out the steps, should you get confused. You can also check out the following YouTube video that isn't quite the exact steps I'm taking, but very close. This video should serve you well, especially if you learn more quickly by observing something being done.

After you gather your ingredients and place them together and make the dough, you may be faced with three options that all in effect do the same thing. How do you know what option you should take?

Sometimes the recipe will tell you. At that point, especially if you're a novice baker, should take its recommendation. If you don't care about how the bread turns out using that option, then make a note of that. It may be that you would like to try another option. By the time you make the bread a second time, you should have enough self-confidence in yourself and familiarity with the steps of baking bread that you'll just fly right through another option.

## THREE WAYS TO PREPARE YOUR DOUGH

Yes, I'm being purposely cryptic about mentioning them because many of us – especially when we're first starting out – don't really want to face the truth. The three options are: autolyze, knead or fold the dough in order to get the yeast working its magic.

Of those three, the one you're probably the most familiar with is the kneading of the dough. The one you probably never heard of before is the autolyze. Believe it or not, despite its scientific-sounding name, it's the easiest option.

### AUTOLYZE: A CONVENIENT, YET EFFECTIVE OPTION

It's a technique that can fit quite nicely works easily into your bread dough recipe. This method aims to ultimately make the dough easier to work with. You'll be able to shape it with ease. Some bread bakers even say the bread rises better when they use the autolyze method.

But don't think for a minute that "ease" equates with cheating on the taste. When you autolyze, you'll also discover your end product, has a better, more appetizing texture and the process brings out more the bread's natural flavor.

And as more than one person has said about this method: "It's deceptively easy."

Here's all you need to do:

**1. Combine the flour and water in a bowl.**

Do not add either the yeast or the salt yet.

**2. Mix this combination until the flour is completely moistened.**

When you're done mixing your dough should have no dry flour left.

**3. Cover the bowl.**

**4. Place it in a warm location.**

That's right. To complete the process, you not only need to find someplace warm and cozy for it, but you need to keep it there for anywhere from twenty minutes to three hours.

Bread bakers call this a resting stage, but to be truthful, the bread is not doing anything but resting. First, by allowing the bread to sit, you're encouraging natural gluten development. It's also during this period that the simple sugars are forming as the starch in the dough breaks down.

And trust me, when you return to check on the dough, even if this is your first loaf of bread you're tackling, you'll notice the difference immediately. It has become smoother and more elastic.

Talk to five different bread bakers, and you'll hear five different ways they use this technique. First, it's guaranteed that not one of them allow the dough to rest the same amount of time. After all, recommendations from 20 minutes to several hours leaves a large hole for your own judgment. And when you're just learning how to do something, the longer it takes for a response, the longer you have to worry if you've done it correctly (at least that's how I am.).

Some professional bakers contend that even a short resting period as twenty minutes is better than skipping this step altogether. Still, recommends that an optimum amount of time is about two to four hours. This is especially true for breads which contain a higher percentage of whole-grain flours.

Here's another aspect of autolyzing you should keep in mind. The time you've allowed the dough to autolyze affects the amount of kneading once the yeast and salt is introduced.

Bottom line, the longer you allow your dough to autolyze the less time you can spend kneading it.

The autolyze process gives the flour an opportunity to hydrate while the proteins present are allowed to bond even before the dough is handled through kneading or folding. This, believe it or not, allows much of the gluten to appear.

Most of the time, the autolyze method is used before you add the yeast and salt to the dough. At this point, the dough doesn't need the yeast. The acidity caused by adding the yeast would only strengthen the dough. You should wait till this step is completed before you add the salt because it too can affect the development of gluten. Salt only tightens the gluten network

If you are aware of what is happening when you do add salt to your dough. The next time you add salt to your dough, be aware that just a small amount of salt can change the dough's texture. It tightens the gluten network. The dough as you mix the salt in becomes more difficult to stretch as you knead it.

If you're not sure exactly what you need to do, check out this YouTube video:

https://www.youtube.com/watch?v=a17Il6F_i8U

This method is usually most when baking sourdough bread, however, it work's in all types of bread. You may want to try it in one of your favorite recipes. You'll notice the difference the moment you start kneading the dough. But more than that, you'll taste the difference as well. Guaranteed.

## THE NEED TO KNEAD

The directions below will help you through your first kneading session. The following directions are specifically for kneading the bread dough by hand. The first thing you'll want to do is to get yourself prepared. This doesn't take long and makes cleaning your hands afterward even easier.

The trick is to get yourself a bowl and rub oil all over it. You're doing this to create a "non-stick" effect so it will be that much easier to get the dough out of the bowl when it's ready.

I know you haven't been looking forward to this step. Many feel that way. But give kneading a chance. For some, they find it enjoyable and even relaxing in an odd sort of way.

However way you eventually end up feeling about kneading, this step doesn't take as long as its reputation would have you believe. By the time you've kneaded and folded your bread according to the specifications of your bread – you'll be surprised at how fast the time has gone by.

Just one more word of caution before we get down to business. Be aware of the height of the surface you'll be using when you knead. You want to avoid straining your back during this time. If at all possible, find a table at which you can extend your arms to knead without your need to hunch over the table itself.

This process really only requires the use of the heels of your hands.

1. You push the dough down with your heels.

2. Place the dough on a lightly four-dusted surface.

3. Dust the dough with a bit of flour as well.

4. Fold what you have in front of you in half.

5. Rotate the dough a quarter of a circle.

This means you'll be turning it to about a 45-degree angle.

6. Now, again using the heels of your hands, push the dough down.

7. If you feel the dough is too sticky, dust it with a bit more flour at your discretion.

This helps to reduce the stickiness. And don't worry. After you've kneaded several loaves of bread, your "desertion," will be simply translated into your intuition.

8. Continue on like this folding, kneading with the heels of your hands and turning, until you've

fulfilled the requirements of the recipe with which you're working

Your recipe will either tell you how many times to knead or to perform this step until your dough gets to be a certain consistency. For most recipes, it takes between 10 and 12 minutes of hand kneading to make sure you've got the gluten working. At this point, you can be confident that you've got the gluten network working throughout the dough.

Still not sure about kneading? Check out this YouTube video:

https://www.youtube.com/watch?v=BiMtyjNK8k0

But, here are a few more ways to be sure that you've kneaded your dough adequately.

**1. Kneading for 10-12 minutes by hand or 8-10 minutes in a mixer are the general standards.**

If you've been massaging the dough for that length of time, you can be pretty confident that you've done your job. Here are a few other things to look for when the dough is beginning to look smooth.

You remember what the dough looked like at the beginning of the process. A lumpy mess almost jaggedly in appearance. Even if you're not sure how many minutes or how many times you knead the bread, if it's looking smooth, you're probably down.

The dough, in addition to being completely smooth, will also be just a bit tacky when you touch it.

## 2. The dough retains its shape.

Perform the lift test on the dough. Take the ball of dough and hold it in your hand. Now hold it in the air for just a few seconds. If you've kneaded it enough the ball will retain its shape. This is the best indication that the gluten is tight and strong.

Should it "sag" between your fingers, then the gluten isn't tight enough yet and you'll have to knead it a few more times.

## 3. The indentation test.

Give that ball of dough a firm jab of your finger. This, of course, creates an indentation in the surface of the dough. If the dough quickly returns to its original position, congratulations, you've kneaded it enough.

If, on the other hand, that impression remains, you need to return to your table and give it a few more turns and punches with the heels of your hands.

## 4. The stretch test.

Break off a piece of the dough – all you'll need is about one the size of a golf ball. Now, you'll stretch it between your fingers. If you can stretch it into a paper thin film without breaking it, you've got a well-kneaded piece of dough. If it breaks, you'll need to go back and work it some more.

## 5. The 'My-arms-are-tired' test.

Oh, so you don't think this is an official test? It is in my kitchen. If you've kneaded the dough the requisite number of times, or throughout the stated time period you've probably done a decent job.

If, in addition, you've run your dough through the tests above and it has come out even close to passing them, you should have no worries that you've got a dough full of fully developed gluten. If, in addition, you've run your dough through the tests above and it has come out even close to passing them, you should have no worries that you've got a dough full of fully developed gluten.

You can stop kneading here with the confidence you've got a loaf of bread in your near future that not only has great texture but is delicious as well.

## THE LAST OPTION: FOLDING THE DOUGH

Remember that dough you left in a warm place when it went through the autolyze step? Yes, that's the one.

The one we just kneaded step by step. Some bakers prefer to knead in that fashion and instead fold the dough. Some recipes, as a matter of fact, call for folding instead of kneading.

When you encounter one of these, and you will sooner or later, here's a quick description of how to perform this step. Just like kneading, it's not as difficult as it sounds. Using this step will also produce an excellent tasting loaf of bread with a delightful texture.

Below is a brief, but accurate description of how to fold your bread dough.

You can start folding your dough about after it has risen for approximately an hour and a half. (Hint: do not sit in the kitchen watching your dough rise during this time. It doesn't sound like an exciting way to spend your time.)

Every good baker acknowledges when they first began working with bread dough, they struggled a bit with this part of the process. So, if you feel like it isn't coming that easy, don't give up. The rewards of making your own bread are far too great to let the lack of a bit of practice scare you away.

Before you even learn the proper method, it's actually good to know why you need to fold the dough. Folding the dough encourages the development of a gluten structure. As you stretch and layer the gluten within that dough, you're making it a more effective to hold both water and air. What you're doing, basically is getting more air into the dough.

Not only that, but the folding action establishes a better "*open crumb structure*" as it's called.

A second reason to fold that dough is to ensure proper distribution of the yeast throughout the loaf. This step also helps to keep the temperature of the dough relatively consistent throughout the entire loaf.

You'll begin the folding process by getting your dough spatula as well as your bread knife. You're going to scrape around the edges of the bowl first, so nothing sticks to it. Now make a "clean" of a fold as possible. You're going to be tempted to tug at it, because of its elasticity, but don't. Allow the dough do all the stretching. Your hands are there only as a pair of assistants, as it were. Right now that might sound strange, but as you perform these folds you'll see exactly what I'm talking about.

Simply pull the side the farthest from you upward and toward yourself. Now fold the dough in half. Moving the bowl about a quarter of a turn, repeat this. Give the bowl a half turn. Perform the same motion. And finally, take the unfolded side of your dough, pull it up from the bottom and then pull it up and over itself.

The bread dough, at this point of the folding process, should feel and look as if it's tight. Not only that but if you touch it at this point, it'll have somewhat of a spring to it.

Not only that but you'll also immediately notice that the dough is not nearly as sticky as it was when you first started working with it.

Put this aside for approximately another hour and a half. You may want to set a timer or the alarm on your smartphone and go about your day. By the time you come back to check on it, the first thing you should notice is the creases in the dough have melded together. This means that the "gluten network" has relaxed. Now it's time to stretch them all over again.

This time you want to be especially careful not to push too hard on the dough or you'll "*de-gas*" it. That would effectively undo the results you received on the first cycle of folding.

Follow the steps outlined above and then cover the bowl. Set your timer or alarm for another forty-five minutes. When that time period is completed return to your loaves. Before you turn them wet your hands. Carefully push down lightly on the dough.

If the dough feels dense, you need to allow it a bit more time to rise. Another half hour would be a good start as an estimate.

If it feels "really" dense, then you need to place your loaves in another location. Start by relocating it to a warmer area of your kitchen. The dough, when it's ready, should feel like a flower garden waterbed. It should have some spring to it and at the same time should leave an imprint.

Once you get to that point, then you can divide the dough. Dividing it, by the way, is the basic first step in shaping them into loaves or rolls. Believe it or not, you're making progress.

What would these instructions be if you couldn't see something similar in action? Yes, another YouTube video if you want to make sure you're on the right track – and quite frankly to show you how ridiculously easy this is:

https://www.youtube.com/watch?v=CQHuWDEo3SA

## DIVIDING THE DOUGH

Now that the yeast has done its duty and the gluten has gotten its spring, it's time for you to take this dough and divide it, so you can begin to shape it the way you want it.

Start by lightly sprinkling it with some all-purpose flour and then scrape around the sides of the bowl. Continue to do this until the dough has come loose from the sides of the bowl. Quickly flip your bowl over. What had been the top of your dough is now sitting on the bottom, just as what had been sitting on the bottom of it is now on type.

Don't worry, yes, it really is supposed to look like a blob. And if you've performed your job correctly, your dough at this point should be sticky – really sticky. Because the dough is so sticky, you'll want to flour not only your hands but the counter workspace as well as your bench knife.

Using your bench knife, you'll cut the dough in half. Make sure you've made a solid cut by pushing the two halves away from each other. In this way, you know that you've cut the dough all the way through.

You'll cut and shape the dough according to the directions of your recipe. While you're doing this, here are some tips to keep in mind to have a perfect size, perfect shapes and delicious tasting rolls and bread.

## 3 TIPS ON DIVIDING YOUR DOUGH

## 1. Use a bench scraper

If you don't have a bench scraper, don't worry. You can still make nice clean cuts into the dough – which is exactly what you want – with a meat cleaver or a sharp, non-serrated knife. Kitchen scissors are also a good tool for the job if you have to divide the bread into smaller pieces.

## 2. Do not use a sawing motion when cutting the dough.

Oh, you'll cut through the dough, all right. But you'll also be slashing the gluten network that you've so lovingly spent developing. You really wouldn't be happy with the results once the dough is baked.

## 3. For best results on equality of size in your dough, weigh each piece.

Of course, you can cut and then hope your eyes are good enough to ensure the pieces are all the same size. But weighing them is a more accurate method. If you find that one is distinctly larger or smaller than the others, then you can cut a chunk off one the other pieces and set it into another piece.

# CHAPTER 6: THE RECIPE FOR A STANDARD LOAF OF BREAD

**INGREDIENTS**

1 package (1/4 ounce) active dry yeast

2-1/4 cups warm water (110° to 115°)

3 tablespoons sugar

1 tablespoon salt

2 tablespoons canola oil

6-1/4 to 6-3/4 cups all-purpose flour

## DIRECTIONS

Dissolve the yeast in warm water in a large bowl.

Add three cups of flour, oil, salt, and sugar. Beat this mixture until it's smooth. Stir in the rest of the flour, a half cup at a time. When you've completed this, you should have a soft dough.

Turn this dough onto a floured surface and then knead it (according to the instructions in the previous chapter) until the dough is smooth and elastic. This should take between 8 to 10 minutes. Put this in a greased bowl, turning the dough once to ensure you've greased the top of the dough along with all the other areas of it. Cover the dough. Place it in a warm place with a paper towel covering the top loosely and allow it to rise until it's about doubled in size. This should take about a one-and-half hour.

At this point in the recipe, you'll want to punch the dough down. Then turn it onto a lightly floured surface. Divide the dough in half. Shape your dough into two loaves. Place these in two greased 9 by 5-inch loaf pans.

Cover these and allow these to rise until they have doubled in size. This should take between 30 to 45 minutes.

Bake these loaves at 375 degrees for approximately 30 to 35 minutes. The crust should be golden brown. Another way of telling the bread is baked right is by tapping on it. It should sound hollow. Remove from the loaves from the pans and place on the wire rack to cool sufficiently. You may not realize that when a recipe calls for cooling bread on a wire rack, this time is actually a part of the baking process. Ironic, I know. If you were to slice that bread immediately after you took it out of the oven, you'd be disappointed.

In order to allow your bread to cool the way, it should you need to quickly take them from the oven and place them on the wire rack.

This was on our list of must-have equipment. If you don't have one, you should, if you can afford it, find an inexpensive one. You may even be able to find a second-hand one at a local thrift store.

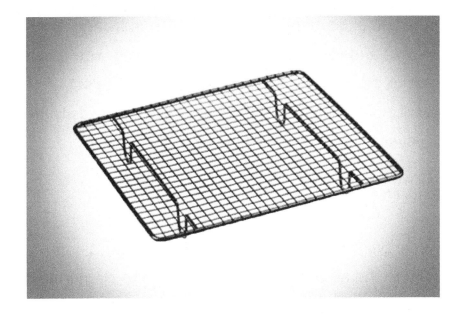

The wire rack allows the air to circulate completely around the loaf which prevents the bread from getting soggy. As the bread cools the water molecules in the dough move outward in an even fashion toward the crust.

What would happen should you get overexcited and cut the bread too soon? The interior of the bread will still be soft. The bread won't slice evenly at all, and the inside will still be gummy and stick to your knife.

It's much better to allow your bread to cool and firm up some before cutting into it.

There are exceptions to this rule of thumb. And that's the rolls and the baguettes. This has to do with a high crust to crumb ratio (who knew?), and there's practically no further internal baking that needs to be achieved once they're taken out of the oven.

*Congratulations!*

You've baked your first two loaves of bread. I can imagine the aroma in your house and the clamoring of your children and spouse on when you can cut the bread, enjoy it with butter or make a sandwich of your dreams.

You'll also discover this makes a great evenly toasted slice of toast to have with your morning coffee.

# CHAPTER 7: RECIPES TO GET YOU STARTED

I've included a few of my favorite recipes. Some of these are my original "starter" recipes, those I used when I was still worried that every loaf of bread or every roll would result in a disaster.

You'll be surprised by the ingredients. Each one is straightforward. But more than that, I've tried to write the directions – the step by step mechanics – of the project in a conversational tone.

I threw out the idea of sounding like a recipe book and adopted the concept that I'm standing next to you in your kitchen explaining the next step you should take. I got the idea from when my mother and grandmother would let me help make bread. They guided me. Never once did they sound like a recipe book.

I'm hoping that helps you connect with the process more than reading sterile "technical" baking copy.

# "IMPOSSIBLE-TO-FORGET" BREAKFAST ROLLS

These "impossible-to-forget" rolls will soon become your "new" favorite rolls. In fact, you'll have trouble not baking them just for breakfast. They have a great, crunchy crust and a delectable soft center.

If that weren't enough, they have walnuts, raisins and pumpkin seed tucked inside.

## INGREDIENTS

**For the Rolls:**

1/2 ounce package active yeast

1 1/2 cup warm water (at 110 ºF)

1/2 teaspoon sugar (granulated)

4 1/2 cups all-purpose flour

1 teaspoon kosher salt

1/2 cup brown sugar

1 tablespoon cinnamon (ground)

1 tablespoon ginger (ground)

4 tablespoons shortening

**For the Filling:**

1 cup raisins (rehydrated in water)

1/2 cup walnuts (chopped) 1/2 cup pumpkin seeds

1/4 cup sesame seeds

1/4 cup sunflower seeds

## Directions

In a large bowl, mix water, sugar, and yeast. Allow the yeast to sit and for five minutes.

Add flour, salt, sugar, shortening as well as cinnamon and ginger.

Mix, preferably in a stand mixer with a dough hook for approximately 12 minutes. You'll know the dough has been mixed enough when it's not excessively sticky.

Put the dough in a greased bowl. Allow this to rise for approximately an hour in a warm, dry place.

Preheat oven to 350 degrees F.

Now, punch the dough down.

 Then divide it into a dozen balls as equal in size as you can get them. Take each ball separately and create a 3 inch long squares. Place the raisin, walnut and seed mixture on top of each dough square. Roll this diagonally and tuck in the sides. Now roll this is the seed mixture coating it and with the seam facing the down, lie it on a parchment sheet lined cookie sheet. Bake for 25 minutes at 350 degrees or until golden brown.

## NAAN

Naan is also knows as the Indian Tandoori bread, which is gaining popularity in the western world fast. It is known for its tender, soft yet crunchy taste and goes well with any type grilled meat.

## INGREDIENTS

1 $1/2$ cups warm water

1 tablespoon sugar

2 teaspoons active dry yeast

1 teaspoon salt

3 cups flour plus a few tablespoons for workspace

## DIRECTIONS

Place the warm water, sugar, and yeast in a large bowl. Allow this to stand for approximately five minutes. When the ingredients begin to get foamy is an indication that the ingredients are ready. Now you can add salt and flour.

Mix these ingredients well. On a floured workspace, knead the dough about 20 times. Form this into a tight ball. Place the dough in a well-greased bowl then cover with a damp cloth.

Place this in a warm location. Allow it to rise for 30 to 45 minutes. Don't expect the dough to rise a lot, but don't worry. It doesn't need to rise much.

Create a floured workspace and turn the dough out on it. Divide this dough into 8 pieces. Using a rolling pin, roll them out, so they are about an eighth of an inch thick.

Grill these on a grill or an electric griddle. If you have neither, you can use a frying pan sprayed with

Turn dough out onto a floured workspace. Divide dough into 8 pieces and roll out with a rolling pin to about 1/8" thick.

Grill naan pieces on a grill or electric griddle. In a pinch, a frying pan sprayed with some nonstick cooking spray. Grill for 1-2 minutes on each side.

Once done, you can even brush the naan with some melted garlic butter to make fresh garlic naan and enjoy it with your tandoori chicken or even with spaghetti and meat sauce.

# FRENCH BREAD

Who said enjoying a fresh French baguette is reserved for special occasions or eating out. With this recipe, you can enjoy one whenever the craving hits.

## INGREDIENTS

2 cups warm water

1 tablespoon yeast

1 tablespoon vegetable oil

1 tablespoon sugar

2 teaspoons salt

5 to 5 $\frac{1}{2}$cups <u>bread flour</u>

**DIRECTIONS**

Dissolve the yeast in warm water – approximately 110 degrees – along with the sugar in a large bowl. Let it set for about 10 minutes.

After that period, add the salt, oil and three cups of flour. Beat this mixture for about two minutes. Stir in two cups of flow to make a stiff dough.

Knead this un5il it's smooth and elastic. This should be about 10 minutes. Place it in a greased bowl. Turn the dough, so all areas of the dough are coated. Cover this. Allow it to rise until it's approximately doubled in size.

At the end of the 10 minutes, punch it down and divide it in half. Shape the dough into two long slender loaves. Grease a French bread pan if you have one, otherwise use a cookie sheet, greased.

Place these two loaves in the plan, making diagonal cuts on top.

Cover this and again let it rise until it's about doubled in size.

Bake at 375 degrees for approximately 30 minutes.

## WHOLE WHEAT BREAD

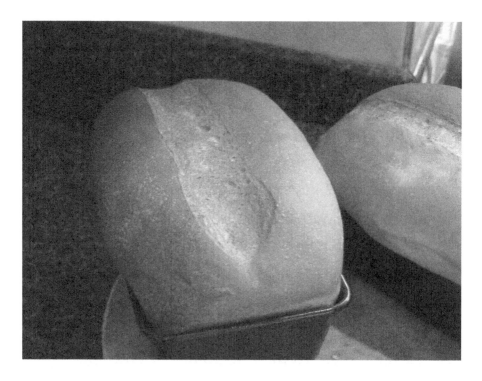

**Ingredients**

2 ³/₄ cups hot water

$^1/_3$ cup olive oil, any oil is fine

$^1/_3$ cup honey

2 tablespoons molasses

1 tablespoon salt, Sea Salt is good

7 $^1/_2$cups of 100% whole grain wheat flour

2 tablespoons dry active yeast

## Directions

Take the hot water, olive oil, honey, molasses and salt into a bowl and mix them thoroughly. Add to this two cups of the wheat flour. This cools the water and you'll now have the warm dough. Then mix in two tablespoons of dry active yeast.

Now add four more cups of the wheat flour. Mix this until it appears that all the ingredients have been evenly distributed throughout the dough. Continue to

Add the flour – a half cup at a time – until your dough no longer sticks to the sides of the bowl.

While the dough won't be clinging to the side of the bowl, it still will be "tacky" when you touch it. You need for the dough to have that consistency to stand up using the least amount of flour. If you can find this, you can be sure you'll have fluffy bread. More than likely you'll use about six and a half cups, but whatever you use, don't put more than 7 ½ cups of flour into this.

When this is done, leave it in the mixer, cover it and allow it to rise for half an hour to 45 minutes. You'll notice the dough has grown, but don't worry if it doesn't double in size. It doesn't need to.

Next, grease two pans. Then, mix the dough one more time. Just long enough to decrease the size of it to near its original size.

Put the dough on your floured work surface. Shape – using your hands is fine – into a ball. Now, take this ball and divide it in half.

When you shape the ball, which is going to be your "loaf" of bread, you start by turning the dough under itself. Do this several times. You'll know when you've completed the shaping process when the sides and ends are well sealed. It will look like an oblong-shaped loaf with both the sides and top looking smooth.

Place the dough in bread pans allow them until they've nearly doubled in size.

Bake in a preheated oven at 350 degrees for about 35 minutes to 40 minutes.

Take the bread out of the oven immediately when it's done baking and transfer it to a wire rack to cool. You can eat it anytime but don't wrap the loaves until they are completely cooled. You can store this bread on the counter in aluminum foil. Don't store it in the refrigerator. It will just harden up.

## PIZZA CRUST

What self-respecting baker can't make a pizza crust?

Well, most people don't look at it that way, but it just may be what your children are thinking. Why not surprise them one evening with a homemade pizza? It would make a great supper or a real treat along with a good Netflix movie.

This recipe calls for bread flour, which will give you a crispy crust. If you prefer a chewier crust, go ahead and substitute all-purpose flour.

**Ingredients**

3 1/2 to 4 cups bread flour, plus more for rolling

1 teaspoon sugar

1 envelope instant dry yeast

2 teaspoons kosher salt

1 1/2 cups water, 110 degrees F

2 tablespoons olive oil, plus 2 teaspoons

**Directions**

In a stand mixer, combine your bread flour, yeast, sugar and kosher salt in the bowl. Turn the mixer on and add the water and two tablespoons of the oil. Mix it until the dough naturally forms into a bow. If the dough feels sticky, add a little more flour, one tablespoon at a time. Keep doing this until the dough is a solid ball.

Should the dough be too dry, then add warm water to the dough. Again you'll want to do this slowly, not more than one tablespoon at a time. Continue to do this until the dough forms a solid ball. Once the dough is in the ball, you'll want to scrape the dough on your lightly floured work surface. Now, knead it into a smooth, firm ball

Grease a large bowl using the two teaspoons of olive oil you've measured out separately.  Place the dough in the bowl, then cover it with a plastic wrap. Place this in a warm location for approximately an hour. This should be sufficient enough time to allow it to double in size.

Once it's doubled in size take the dough and turn it out onto your lightly floured work surface. Divide the ball into two equal pieces. Cover each of these pieced with a clean cloth and allow them to rest for approximately ten minutes.

At the end of ten minutes, roll the dough out using a rolling pin. You'll want to roll the pin over all parts of the dough ball until you get to the right height you want.

You'll then top with your favorite pizza combination or find one online. You'll normally bake this for 30 t0 40 minutes at 450 degrees.

# CHAPTER 8: TIPS FOR MAKING PERFECT BREAD DOUGH: WHAT SERIOUS BAKERS MAY NOT TELL YOU

There's nothing more frustrating than doing something, like baking bread and having it not turn out right and you standing there having not a clue as to what you did wrong.

I know that because when I first started, that was me. I would prepare my taste buds for a great-tasting warm piece of bread or a roll only to find that I did something wrong. The sad part is, I didn't have enough experience to know what I did to cause such a disaster.

That's why I'm including this chapter. It provides you with tips on may have gone wrong when you end up with a botched batch of bread. This by no means covers all of the possible problems one could face, but does provide you solution to some of the more common ones. Hopefully, this will save you from drinking endless cups of coffee plowing through websites searching for what went awry.

# PROOF YOUR YEAST

I see you nodding your head agreeing with me, but I also can read your eyes and can see you have no idea what that phrase means. Nor should you, unless you've worked with yeast in the past.

When someone recommends to proof the yeast, what you're going to do is to prove that it's alive. What you're really going to test is that the yeast is eating sugar and giving off bubbles of carbon dioxide . . . because . . . well, that's the job of yeast.

Let's start off by saying that if you're using a new packet of yeast and the use-by date is well into the future, it's not necessary to proof it, especially if you're a veteran baker.

Even if the date's on the package is good, and you've never used yeast before, it might be a good idea to proof it anyway. In this way, you will have a baseline of experience to know what should happen if the yeast is doing its job.

If you found some older yeast stuck in the back of a kitchen cabinet and you're wondering if you can use it, then by all means proof it.

If the recipe you're using directs you to place all your ingredients including the yeast and mix them together using a mixer then simple warm up a portion of that water to about 140 degrees Fahrenheit.

Don't worry over the exact temperature of the water. If you think it feels warm and comfortable, then it'll be a good environment for the yeast. To this, add just a pinch of sugar and squirt of honey or a splash of maple syrup. You want to give the yeast just enough of what it needs to wake up and well, smell the sweetness and do its thing.

Mix this all together. Wait 10 to 15 minutes. If at the end of that time period, the mixture is bubbly and foamy with a dense head on top, you've good working yeast, and you're good to go. If there are no bubbles or foam, then the yeast is not working. It's no longer alive. And yes, it's time to buy more.

## DON'T SCOOP THE FLOUR OUT OF THE CONTAINER WITH THE MEASURING CUP

Of course, you'll be tempted to do this, but if you use this method, you'll discover that you've used too much flour. The end result will be a heavy loaf of bread.

Instead, use a spoon to take the flour from the container and place into the measuring cup. Then be sure not to tap or shake the cup in order to try to get as much as possible in there. Once it's filled, simply level the top of the measure cup with a flat edge.

## DON'T SLICE THE BREAD IMMEDIATELY AFTER TAKING IT FROM THE OVEN.

Wait a minimum of fifteen minutes before slicing. By doing this, you run far less of a chance of tearing the crust.

If you're baking a quick bread, this is a bread that has cornstarch acting as the leavening agent; it advised that wait until the next day to cut them. (Like anyone in the house can smell the bread and wait. It'll be tough enough for you and your family to wait the fifteen minutes.

## YOUR BREAD IS BROWNING TOO QUICKLY

Once the bread is brown enough, take it out of the oven and make a tent out of aluminum foil to put over the top of the loaf. Place it back in the oven until it's done baking.

## WAS THE DOUGH KNEADED ENOUGH?

As you look over your little bundle of love, wondering if you've kneaded the dough enough, you can find out relatively easily. Simply break off a small, piece of dough, about the size of a walnut. Stretch this, much like you would a deflated balloon or a piece of bubble gum. If the dough doesn't tear easily and it possesses a visible translucent sheath, then it's kneaded well enough. That translucent film is often called the gluten window.

Using a bread-baking machine? Then you'll want to check the progress of the bread's first cycle of kneading.

The method of measuring flour as well as its moisture content is a known factor n affecting the dough's consistency. After five or ten minutes of the machine's running in the knead cycle, take the lid off the machine.

At this point, you should find a soft, tacky ball of dough. If it's still dry and stiff, then you'll need to add liquid to it. How much? Add only a half or one tablespoon at a time...

If on the other hand, you discover your dough is too wet then you should add flour to the mixture – again one tablespoon at a time until the mixture is the tacky ball you need.

## CAN YOU REHEAT HOMEMADE BREAD?

Yes, you can, and you'll be glad you did. Turn the oven to 350 degrees Fahrenheit. If you're reheating an entire loaf, you'll want to wrap this in aluminum foil; and place it in the oven for an average of 15 to 20 minutes. Treat slices of bread and rolls in the same manner for reheating.

## ALL INGREDIENTS SHOULD BE AT ROOM TEMPERATURE BEFORE YOU MIX THEM

That's right. Before you mix your ingredients together, make sure they are all at room temperature. You'll want them to sit on your kitchen counter or your table prior to you placing them together.

## CRUMBLING BREAD? WHAT COULD POSSIBLY GO WRONG?

Actually, several things could cause your bread to crumble excessively. Below is a list of several troubleshooting steps to take if your bread is too crumbly.

1. **The right kind of flour.**

This is where you begin looking. It really does matter that you use bread flour when the recipe calls for flour. Your average all-purpose or self-rising flour are not going to hold a candle to the bread flour. I

## 2. Use about a quarter cup less flour.

You may have accidentally used too much flour, which can dry out the dough and cause the crumbling.

## 3. Add warm water while the bread is mixing.

If the dough feels dry while you're mixing it go ahead and slowly add water into the mixture. Don't add more than one teaspoon at a time and see how the dough reacts. If the dough still seems dry, go ahead and do it again.

## 4. When the dough has doubled in size, punch it down.

Sometimes your bread gets crumbly when it more than doubles in size before you get the chance to punch it down. The dough shouldn't grow to more than twice its size before you punch it down.

## 5. Use a serrated knife to slice your bread.

It's very possible that your crumbly dough has nothing to do with the baking process. It could be you're not be cutting it with the right type of knife. If you have a knife with a serrated edge, cut your dough with that to see if that helps the situation at all.

## WHAT ABOUT GLUTEN-FREE DOUGH?

The rise of celiac disease, caused by even a bit of gluten in a person's system opened up an entirely new set of circumstances when it comes to making gluten-free bread. At the same time, the two diets, the Keto Diet and the Paleo diet rose to new levels of usage. Many have given or are giving up gluten or cutting carbs, which make traditional bread totally off limits.

In fact, there are several ideas about the best way to do this.

I'll talk about several, and you can look for more if you like. The one thing you should know that there are more choices to gluten bread than ever before. And what we're talking about here is really only a drop in the bucket, as they say.

First, let's start with the challenge of converting a recipe that is made with wheat flour into one that any celiac would love eat.

One time, not so many years ago making that conversion involved eliminating the wheat flour and replacing it with a ratio of flours that most people had never heard of. Sure they may have read some of the names on certain labels, but for the most part, these were flours that they were definitely unfamiliar with. Even today many people would prefer not to work with five different kinds of flour in one recipe.

And today, you can actually do that. This is the easiest and cleanest way of converting a recipe. You simply replace the flour of the traditional bread with gluten-free all-purpose flour.

Total up the amount of flour in the original recipe and use that amount of the gluten-free all-purpose flour. Be sure not to add more xanthan gum or guar gum if the recipe calls for it. If you retain these two flours it will only make your flour gummy.

Converting your recipe in this manner, you may need to add more baking powder. Don't be afraid to add from half a teaspoon to a full teaspoon to the recipe. That means if the wheat-based flour recipe requires one teaspoon and you think you need more you can put at most two teaspoons in the recipe.

When you do this, however, just be sure to make a note of the optimum amount of baking powder you used. That way, you're not forever fumbling with those numbers.

# CHAPTER 9: BAGUETTES, BOULES, BAGELS AND MORE: WHO WOULD HAVE THOUGHT THERE WERE SO MANY TYPES OF BREADS?

We all have a love affair with bread.

And it didn't just start with this century, nor the last one. I don't have any proof, but I think it started with our cave people ancestors. Whoever of them was the first to discover what could be done with wheat was a genius, of course, but should be revered with changing the world just like the first of our ancestors who created the wheel.

By the way, we've gotten creative with the different types of breads we've created and loved, it's not likely that the love affair is going to end anytime soon. This chapter is dedicated to brief descriptions of only a few types of breads. Given enough time and patience, you'll be able to make all of these. And you'll become lucky enough, that means, that you can eat them warm.

Here are just a few of the different types of breads. I've included ones you're probably familiar with – at least you probably know their names. I've also included several you may never have heard of before. Now, that's where the fun come in discovering new ways to use your dough and your equipment.

**Arepa.** This is a bread that has a texture, not unlike a soft tortilla, but it differs in that it's thicker than tortillas. And that comparison to tortillas is no coincidence; it's highly popular in South America. Made from "maize" flour, it is best when eaten in a sandwich with meat and cheese. And yes, it is gluten-free.

**Baguette.** Probably at its height of popularity right now, this is a type of French bread. It's typically characterized by its elongated tubular shape. It offers a crunchy crust that pairs perfectly with the soft texture of the inside of the loaf.

While the length of these loaves can be up to two-feet, you can find them – and make them – in a wide variety of lengths. You probably know them best from making sandwiches, they are also a great accompaniment to soups and salads as well. And don't let anyone fool you. Of course, they're awesomely delicious with warm butter spread over them. But these babies are tasty enough to stand alone – without butter.

**Bahn Mi.** Meet the Vietnamese cousin to the baguette. It's made with a blend of wheat and rice flour. Like the Arepa from South America, it's the go-to bread to eat when you eat traditional Vietnamese sandwiches.

**Bagels.** Ah! Here's one of those breads that need no introduction. America's love affair with the bagel has been blossoming for decades, and it's only getting more intense. One of the reasons is its unique texture. A tough, chewy bread, it makes an awesome sandwich as well as a stand-alone bread. The choice is yours.

And that one-of-a-kind texture comes from the way it's baked. Made with yeast dough, bagels are rolled and then they're boiled—yes, boiled – before they're baked in the oven. And of course, the various flavors of this bread are endless.

**Bialy**. Here's another bread that you may not have heard of. In a way, it's similar to the bagel; it's round and chewy. Instead of a hole, like the bagel, the bialy has a small indentation in the center. The indentation is then filled with such ingredients as poppy seeds and onions before you bake it to give its delicious flavor. Just as an aside, the bialy got its name because it was first made in Bialystok, Poland.

**Breadsticks.** The ubiquitous nature of the breadstick is proof how much we love our bread. From the finest of restaurants around the globe to the pizza place up the street, there probably isn't an eatery that doesn't serve them.

These are thin, long pieces of bread. The unique fact about breadsticks you might not have known? They're baked for a long time so the sticks can keep longer before they get eaten.

**Brioche.** You've probably seen this type of bread and without a doubt eaten it, even if you didn't call it brioche. It's a sweet, glazed roll that contains a rich flavor More often than not it's eaten with breakfast. It's easy to make by combing yeast and butter with eggs. After it's done baking, you glaze it with an egg wash. You may find that at times, brioche is flavored with the addition of almonds.

**Challah.** A traditional Jewish bread, challah gets its unique appearance because it's braided before being baked. The bread has a nice, sweet taste to it and is more often than not baked with yeast, eggs, flour, and honey. Now you can see where it gets that sweetness from.

**Ciabatta.** This is an Italian bread which in the last 20 years or so has become popular. It has dense crumbs with a hard and crisp crust.

The most common way it's made is with wheat and flavored with olive oil and rosemary and at times other seasons. As soon as it comes to cornbread. Cornbread is made by baking corn that has been ground down into a meal. Egg and buttermilk are often combined with the cornmeal before baking, making cornbread very cake-like in texture and taste. Cornbread can be very dense and crumby.t of the oven; it's dusted. This bread is a favorite for Panini sandwiches because it toasts well.

**Cornbread**. This is another popular bead. Cornbread is essential made by baking corn ground into meal. You'll probably see egg and buttermilk added to the meal before it's baked. This makes the texture almost cake-like. It can also be a dense and crumbly bread.

**Croissant.** Who doesn't melt like butter on a hot slice of bread when they bite into a croissant? Flakey, buttery and very, very rich. Need we say any more why they're still popular after all these years? And that crescent moon shape, well that just adds to their charm.

A croissant is a French roll. You make it by baking puff pastry and yeast dough together in several layers. While normally considered a breakfast pastry, they can be eaten any time throughout the day. And if you've never tasted a chocolate croissant, you're in for a new taste delight. Believe it or not, a chocolate croissant is easy enough to make. Simply drop a piece of dark chocolate into the dough before you bake it.

**Cracker**. From Croissant to cracker. What a change of pace. We all know what a cracker is. It's just a small piece of very crisp bread, made with flour, salt, water and some type of baking mixture. You probably don't think of them as bread, because they're made minus the yeast.

**Crouton**. You are most familiar with the crouton, no doubt, as those crispy, crunchy Croutons. You are most familiar with the crouton, no doubt, as those crispy, crunchy bread squares topped with your salad that are begging you to pour more salad dressing on them.

These delicious squares just illustrate all the more our love affair with bread. They are in essence stale bread, cut into cubes. They're then seasoned and baked a second time and poof! They've found a new life on salads and in soups.

**English Muffin.** A round yeast roll, the English muffin is most known as the bread of choice for many to hold their breakfast sandwich. And believe It or not, it's very often made by cooking the dough on a griddle. If you've ever had a crumpet, then you know that the muffin can be every bit as dense as its cousin. It is a delight for many due to the fact that it's filled with air pockets. Many of us love the way those pockets become the perfect depositories for melted butter.

**French Bread.** There's hardly anything better than warm French bread. It makes a special Friday night dinner out even more memorable.

But don't think for a moment you can't enjoy this taste at home fresh from your oven. When you've succeeded in making French bread, then you can bake your own baguettes, as well as rolls and boules.

If your mouth is already watering just thinking about the crust, then consider its second texture, that airy dough, and a rich, nutty taste. This makes French bread the perfect accompaniment for all of your meals – yes even breakfast.

**Focaccia**. This bread, originating from of Italy, is flat, relatively speaking. This is because it's not kneaded prior to its being baked. While not considered a flatbread, because it does contain yeast, which gets it to rise slightly. If you've yet to try it, you'll love its flavor. And if you're wondering how it retains that moisture, the secret is to brush olive oil over it before you bake it.

**Fruit bread**. You can find this type of bread in just about any type of variety. In addition to the dried fruit, there are at times nuts in the bread as well. One of the most popular is banana bread.

It very often is prepared more like a cake than a bread; the first difference is the dough is baked in a pan, rather than a loaf. And if you're waiting for it to rise, you'll be waiting a long time. The mixture that composes this bread has no yeast.

**Hot Cross Buns**. Best known as a staple for many during the Easter holiday, hot cross buns are sweet rolls made with yeast and raisins. They get their name from the cross that is cut into the dough many times before being baked.

**Italian**. In this bread, water is mixed into the dough instead of the customary milk. The result is a crusty yeast loaf that has a satisfying chewing crust and a soft center. You can usually distinguish it from French bread immediately, just on its appearance. Italian bread is usually baked in shorter and wide loaves than its French cousin, or you may just as readily find it in boules

**Matzo**. This bread is a flatbread without any yeast. These two facts alone give it a crisp and crunchy texture, not unlike crackers and most associated with the Passover holiday.

**M'smen.** Traditionally a Moroccan flatbread, this bread is considered a part of a breakfast meal. It has a flaky texture as well a wonderfully, buttery flavor.

**Naan.** Another type of flatbread, this one originally from the Middle East. Think pita bread without the pocket. The dough is combined with the leavening and then baked. The authentic bread is made in a clay oven. It's topped with a variety of items, including butter, spiced vegetables, garlic or cheese.

**Panettone.** This is a traditional Italian Christmas bread. It's unique in that the dough is cured for several days before you add a host of candied fruits, raisins, and lemon zest. When the bread is completed, it's a tall loaf with a light texture.

**Paratha**. This is another Indian flatbread that is like naan. Prepared with wheat flour, it's fried in oil and then served stuff a wide variety of foods.

**Poori.** Another type of Indian flatbread, this one made with whole wheat flour and that is combined with salt and water. Fried in oil, the bread when finished resembles a "puffy pillow."

**Popover**. You've probably heard the term, even if you don't know exactly what a popover is. In essence, it's a dough whose ingredients include egg batter being poured into muffin tins. The result is a crispy and light roll with a hollow interior. Why are they called popovers? The named is associated with the method used to cook these rolls. The batter pops over the edge of the muffin tins.

**Potato Bread.** It should be no surprise to you that potato bread was first made in Ireland where the Irish replaced a large part of a read recipe calling for regular flour with mashed potatoes. This was done when a mashed potato was substituted for flour in the baking it. This gives the bread a denser texture than a flour-made bread and also contributes to its one-of-a-kind taste.

**Puff Pastry**. You're familiar with this pastry and probably have had a love affair with it at some point of time, even though you may not have known what it was called. It's made by combining ordinary wheat dough with butter. You roll it until the dough many, many times. What you get is a pastry that is miraculously flaky with amazingly buttery taste. How can you go wrong with this type of bread?

**Pretzel.** This "bread" is at the other end of the spectrum from puff pastry. This is a hardy bread, made by taking yeast dough and rolling it into a long tube. You then twist it and knot it into that unique pretzel shape. Just like puff pastry, you'll find it difficult to resist.

**Pumpernickel.** This bread is, in reality, a mixture of sourdough and crushed rye grains. It's covered before being baked at a low temperature for a long period of time. It's unique in that it comes in many colors from brown to black. You'll usually find it in your local deli on your favorite sandwich.

**Rye.** Made from rye flour –which like pumpernickel can be anywhere from light to dark in color. The color depends on the density of the bread. The flavor of this bread is stronger than wheat and is a denser bread than wheat.

**Marble Bread**. Can't decide between pumpernickel and rye? Then marble bread has your name written all over it. This bread is really two varieties of bread twisted to create that swirl pattern that's associated with it. The two pieces of bread are pumpernickel and rye dough. The twisted dough is baked in dense loaves and outside of the grocery store, you're more than likely to find this bread in delicatessens.

**Scones**. This delicious snack, may not be considered a bread by some. But when it's called a bread, it's classified as a "quick bread." If you're thinking about make your own scone, you'll need the following ingredients, flour, baking soda, eggs, butter, and milk. When you bake these ingredients you'll find you have a dense and dry bread that has an unusually hard crust. You can enjoy them for breakfast and slather them with butter, cream cheese or honey. Many times individuals eat them at their favorite coffee shop with blueberries or raisins already baked into it.

**Soda bread.** No one knows for sure; it's possible that it gets its time because instead of baking with yeast, you put baking soda into it. If you've never tasted it, you're missing a real taste treat. It's sweet and has a delicious light texture. And then to add to its great taste, you'll often see it with nuts or raisins baked into the door.

**Sourdough.** This bread receives its name from its taste. Sourdough is baked using specific bacteria that produce lactic acid. It's the lactic acid that gives the bread it's slightly tart to taste. Most forms of this bread will have a deliciously crispy crust with a softer, even crumbly inside.

**White bread.** Ahh. What many of us think of classic white bread isn't really classic at all. It's actually one of the new kids on the block when it comes to breads. That's because it's made with bleached, chemically refined white flour something only fairly recently commercial bakers have been able to do. The refined white flour is also why it has its white color. In contrast, whole wheat bread is made from unrefined wheat flour.

Here are three top websites that shows all the recipes for the bread I just mentioned above. Enjoy!

https://www.breadexperience.com/

http://allrecipes.com/recipe/220619/real-homemade-bagels/

http://artisanbreadbaking.com/bread/french_baguettes/

# CHAPTER 10: GLUTEN FREE FLOURS AND BREAD: WHAT YOU NEED YOU NEED TO KNOW AS A BREAD BAKER

As little as twenty years ago, most of us had never heard of gluten, let alone worry if it were found in the foods we eat. Even the medical establishment faced with the question of whether a patient may have celiac disease, the disorder which makes it impossible to digest gluten, laughed at the idea.

But even then, it was beginning to gain notoriety in other regions of the world. The problem grew fast enough that the World Health Organization had a label for food manufacturers to place on their packages for all their gluten-free foods.

In the United States, only one percent of the population has been diagnosed with celiac disease yet nearly 33 percent of us – that's one-third of the population is watching its consumption of gluten.

And as more people learn about the potential effects of gluten, the number may indeed increase. Certainly, it's hard to see where it will become the demand of the majority of the people in this country, but it's always good to know a little about it. Especially if someone in your family should develop an intolerance to it.

Here are a few facts that you may already know about gluten, but is essential to review.

## DOES GLUTEN HAVE A PURPOSE IN BREAD DOUGH?

While those living the gluten-free lifestyle would love to shout no, this substance *does* play an important role in bread. It creates strong, sticky and most importantly an elastic texture of the dough. These bonds are the essence of the dough's stretchy qualities.

Think about how a pizza is made. You know the fun part, where you get to see the pizza bakers toss the pressed out round pieces of dough into the air and actually swirl it around. As they do that, the pizza rounds seem to grow in size magically.

Only it's not magic; it's the gluten in the dough.

# GLUTEN HELPS THE DOUGH TO RISE.

That's not the only role that gluten plays in bread dough. This substance is an active partner when combined with yeast in helping the dough rise. The water you add to the flour, in fact, acts upon the development of that gluten network we've talk about occasionally throughout this book.  That, in turn, helps to create a chewier dough.

The other activity that helps the gluten work in the dough is the amount of kneading that's performed on the dough. The more you knead, the more developed the gluten network becomes. That's good news for those of us who love the one-of-a-kind texture of fresh bread, but not so good for a person who has celiac disease.

The yeast gives off a gas, which has no place to go and is trapped in the sheets of the gluten molecules, which in turn, causes the dough to rise.

The first thing you need to know, that even within breads that contain gluten, you may find that different types of flour are needed depending on the purpose of the dough. Different wheat flours produce different amounts of gluten development.

Bead flour, for example, is capable of producing a generous amount of gluten. Cake flour, on the other hand, contains lower levels of gluten. Cake flour is not as chewy as pizza or bread. Yet, it still has enough gluten to keep the baked cake from crumbling.

And when you compare the two of these to pie crusts, the amount of gluten appears almost negligible. Pie crusts though have an abundance of shortening with only a small amount gluten. That's what makes the crusts flaky and tender.

The point of all of this explanation is simple. Gluten is necessary to regular bread dough. You can't skimp on it or even more drastically, simply eliminate it. You'll be disappointed. That doesn't mean there are no methods you can use to adjust the recipe to make a gluten-free creation your family and friends will appreciate.

The easiest method is to simply buy or make gluten-free flour.

This is easy enough and is really all you need to do is coat some food in flour before you sauté it. But if you're serious about baking then you'll want to check out the different types of gluten-free flours. And you'll want to experiment with the types you do pair together.

Let's say though you have a want to make a gluten-free. Do you know what your options are in creating a dough that's gluten-free and actually tastes good?

Your first option is, of course, to replace the entire amount of flour in the recipe with gluten-free all-purpose flour. And that gives you a decent tasting bread without the gluten. And for a while, that may be exactly what you want to stick with, especially if baking hadn't been a large part of your skill set before this.

## THE OPTIMAL WAY TO SUBSTITUTE

When you go this route, you may think that just scooping out a cup for gluten-free bread in place of the regular flour is what you do. Of course, you could do that, but you'll be pleased – and your family much happier with the bread – if you either weigh the flour or use metric measures to ensure accuracy.

Believe me; this is more than mere quibbling about methods. You can try it all three ways to see firsthand the difference not only in taste but texture as well. If you're just going to use a measuring cup, you'll discover that any number of mitigating factors may cause a difference in measurement.

Let's say you just scoop a cup of gluten-free flour. Some of the factors that could change the amount of flour you put in your recipe include the moisture in the air, whether the flour was compacted is it lying in the cup looking light and airy. Even the way you scoop that flour may have an influence on the amount in that cup.

Consider investing in a scale that is capable of weighing items as heavy as eleven pounds. This is so much more accurate, and you'll find by using this form of measurement will bring greater success to all of your baking projects.

Weighing and using metric measures will give you the most consistent results every time. When you use a measuring cup, the moisture in the air, the way you scoop the flour, and whether it was compacted or light and airy changes day to day. A scale never lies! Buy a kitchen scale that goes up to 11 pounds, and it will work for every project your kitchen with astounding consistency.

Before you convert your recipe, take a good look at the measurement it calls for. I'm going to let you in on a secret. The al- important number to keep in mind is 120. That's 120 grams, and it represents the weight of just about every all-purpose flour in the United States.

Knowing this makes converting your recipe super easy. Just use 120 grams of gluten-free flour in its place, you should be just fine. And just so you know, you can simply look at this simple conversion chart I made.

| Portion of a cup of | Weight of a cup of |
| --- | --- |

| all-purpose flour | all-purpose flour |
|---|---|
| 1 cup | 120 grams |
| ¾ cup | 90 grams |
| ½ cup | 60 grams |
| 1/3 cup | 37 1/2 grams |
| ¼ of a cup | 30 grams |
| 2 tablespoons | 15 grams |

As you get more familiar with baking and working with gluten items, in particular, you may want to buy the individual types of gluten-free flours and create your own mix.

As you learn how to play with the gluten-free types of flour to create the perfect loaf or rolls that your family loves, here are some types of how to handle and bake the dough. You need to be aware that your dough, in many ways, ends up fundamentally different from dough with gluten.

## BAKE YOUR DOUGH IN CONTAINERS THAT HAVE WALLS.

If you recall, many times when you're baking a baguette or a boule that contains gluten, you'll place the raw dough onto a cookie sheet before putting it into an oven. But that's not a good decision when it comes to gluten-free baking.

Because this dough lacks gluten, the loafs and rolls won't hold their shape well. Instead, you'll have to give them a structure to keep the dough "in its place," so to speak. Baked the bead in tradition bread loaf pans or even Bundt pans. You can also use muffin pans for the rolls.

## ADD GUM TO YOUR FLOUR.

No, it's not the kind of gum, you pop into your mouth and chew, but the effect of this baking gum is similar. You may decide to add xanthan gum or guar gum to replace the elasticity that the gluten normally provides.

How much? Many bakers say that for every cup of gluten-free flour the recipe calls for you to add between 2 to 3 teaspoons of gum for bread and pizza dough. If you're making a cake, you'll only need to add about one teaspoon of the gum.

## ADD PROTEIN TO YOUR FLOUR.

Another method of compensating for the lack of elastic in your due is to add protein to your flour. You can easily do this by replacing that half of cup of water the recipe calls for with an egg or liquid egg whites.

## BRING OUT YOUR FAVORITE RECIPES AND ADAPT THEM

This is a brilliant idea. Then the entire family can still enjoy the same type of bread. Don't get upset if you don't get the recipe tweaked on the first run-through. It'll take several times of adjusting and readjusting the recipe before you have it to your liking. I know one of my friends did this, and she actually dedicated her entire weekending adapting her favorite bread recipe to gluten-free. She allowed me to taste the final creation – and it was amazingly delicious.

Just take your time and enjoy yourself.

## IF YOU'RE LOOKING FOR SOMETHING NEW IN GLUTEN-FREE BAKING?

Then let your fingers do the walking through many of the gluten-free cookbooks available online today. You can find them through your e-reader apps or through good old-fashioned cookbooks. Between your growing experience and the increasing demand for gluten-free recipes, you'll be surprised at how many new recipes are out there. You can also bet that the number will continue to grow through the next couple of years. Take advantage of such a flood of resources.

And remember, if you don't like how a recipe turned out you can adapt it to meet your unique needs and tastes.

## THE ISSUE OF CROSS-CONTAMINATION.

For that one percent of the population who has celiac disease, living with the fear of cross-contamination can be difficult. Those who have this disorder or are severely intolerable to gluten, sometimes find that even if their bread was baked with utensils that touched gluten, were placed on wooden cutting boards that touched wheat or had any other contact at all, could cause symptoms to flare up.

You can probably see where I'm going here. The first rule of thumb is to never use the same surface for gluten-free and gluten breads. Even the smallest of particles left behind can play havoc with the digestive system for some people.

The wooden cutting board is the most glaring example of this. Regardless of how well you clean it, you'll never be able to remove all gluten particles. This means you'll always have the potential for cross-contamination. It's much easier and less worrisome if you have a set of dedicated tools and utensils you use only when you're working with gluten-free breads. This is the only way you can be sure that cross contamination is not an issue.

## KEEP YOUR GLUTEN-FREE FLOUR IN THE REFRIGERATOR OR THE FREEZER.

This might not be as vital if you're only buying small amounts of it, but if you buy this flour in bulk, as many do it's almost mandatory. Of course, they stay fresher longer and work the way they were intended to. If you do freezer or refrigerate them, take them from the cold and allow them to come to room temperature prior to baking with them.

> **MAKE SURE THE FLOUR YOU'RE USING IS INDEED GLUTEN-FREE.**

This piece of advice may seem silly, but there's a growing number of type of flour available it seems every day. Many of them may "sound" as if they should be gluten-free, but aren't. Here are the most common types of flour you encounter that ARE NOT gluten-free, even though they sound like they should be.

# Types of Flour that Sound as if They Should be Gluten-Free But Are Not! Do Not Substitute these in your Recipes!

| | |
|---|---|
| **All-purpose** | Plain |
| **Bulgar** | Sauce |
| **Bread** | Self-rising |
| **Brown** | Semolina |
| **Cake** | Spelt |
| **Durham** | Triticale |
| **Granary** | Wheaten corn flour |
| **Graham** | Wholemeal flour |
| **Kamut** | Spelt flour |

# CONCLUSION

Ask five different people who bake bread, and you're sure to receive five different answers. For some, it's all about their family's health. For others, it's about saving money, and for still others, they bake bread to ensure that their children who may be gluten intolerant can enjoy tasting good bread.

For me, it's all those things and one more. Baking bread, by hand without using a bread maker makes me feel like a kid again, standing next to my grandmother and my mom, while they took the time and energy to give their family something extra.

Baking bread is all about watching my children gather around me during the process, asking a myriad of questions about the process – but more importantly beg me to tell them stories about their grandmother and their greatma.

And I'd be lying that much about what I love about baking bread is the way a freshly baked loaf of bread makes my house smell, that welcoming type of invitation that is only rivaled in hospitality by the smell of soup on a winter's day

And I sincerely hope I was able to show you the techniques of baking bread, so one day, you may enjoy any or all of the experiences I've mentioned if you desire.

But more than anything else, I hope I was able to show you how excited I am about the process, how much I love it and how passionate I am about baking bread. If you're looking for a hobby, I hope you consider this one.

If you're looking to improve your health, I hope you considering baking bread as that first step toward a new healthier YOU!

If you're seeking to reconnect with your past or make stronger ties with your children, I can't think of a more delicious way in which to do so!

Bake your heart out!

# LAST WORDS

Hopefully, in this book, I was able to give you a good general overview of the basic bread making for all beginners. Remember to follow the directions I provided accurately and you will see that making delicious bread at home is a very easy or simple process, with some effort and careful measurement of all the ingridients, you will see your bread rising with pride.

I wanted to thank you for buying my book; I am neither a professional writer nor an author, but rather a person who always had the passion for baking since childhood when I used smell my grandma's delicious bread baking every morning. In this book, I wanted to share my knowledge with you, as I know there are many people who share the same passion and drive as I do. So, this book is entirely dedicated to YOU my readers.

Despite my best effort to make this book error free, if you happen to find any errors, I want to ask for your forgiveness ahead of time.

Just remember, my writing skills may not be best, but the knowledge I share here is pure and honest.

If you thought I added some value and shared some valuable information that you can use, please take a minute and post a review on wherever you bought this book from. This will mean the world to me. Thank you so much!!

Lastly, I wanted to thank my four wonderful children, Jacob, Rob, Chris and Jennifer and my dear husband Bill for all their help and support throughout this book, without them, this book would not have been possible.

Thank you once again and be safe.

Made in the USA
Middletown, DE
08 February 2019